Texting Women

7 SIMPLE STEPS FROM TEXT TO SEX

By
Felicia Vine

Legal Notes

No part of this publication may be reproduced or transmitted in any form or by any means, mechanical or electronic, including photocopying and recording, or by any information storage and retrieval system, without permission, in writing, from the author.

All attempts have been made to verify information provided in this publication. Neither the author nor the publisher assumes any responsibility for errors or omissions of the subject matter herein. This publication is not intended for use as a source of legal or accounting advice. The Publisher wants to stress that the information contained herein may be subject to varying state and/or local laws or regulations. All users are advised to retain competent counsel to determine what state and/or local laws or regulations may apply to the user's particular business.

The purchaser or reader of this publication assumes responsibility for the use of these materials and information. Adherence to all applicable laws and regulations, federal, state, and local, governing professional licensing, business practices, advertising, and all other aspects of doing business in the United States or any other jurisdiction is the sole responsibility of the purchaser or reader

The author and Publisher assume no responsibility or liability whatsoever on the behalf of any purchaser or reader of these materials for injury due to use of any of the methods contained herein. Any perceived slights of specific people or organizations are unintentional.

Copyright © 2016 Felicia Vine

Introduction

Texting is something that has not been around for a long amount of time, and yet it seems like everyone knows how to text from your grandma to your younger brother and so much more. If you have a phone, you will probably need to use texting at some point or another. While this guidebook is going to spend most of its time talking about using texting in order to get the attention of a girl you like and to get her to contact you back, there are quite a few benefits of texting that can occur when you use it properly. Some of the great benefits that come with texting include:

— Time saver—this is a great idea to use if you do not have the time that is needed in order to have a full conversation. This would be a great idea if you are trying to just ask a few questions to confirm something. It is a good way to break the ice when you are trying to keep the conversation going, but the two of you just met and do not have many topics to talk about as of yet.

— Discretion—texting is one of the most discreet mode of communication. You will be able to text the woman you are interested in no matter what time and even if they are busy with something else. You can ask a question, get a conversation started, or send some other message without having to worry about what the other person is doing. If they are busy, they can wait to get and respond to the message until later; if they have time they will be able to talk and no one will be able to tell anything.

— Easier to use—when you are just meeting someone else, it is easy to become scared about what they will think about you. You might get nervous during the first conversation and the whole think will stall. This does not spell out very good things when you are first starting out, even if it is like this because you are nervous. With texting, you can take a moment to think without feeling pressured and the conversation can keep on going for a long time.

— Conversation starter—if you have been talking with a woman for some time, you might find that you have learned quite a few things in the process. This means that you will be able to use the things you have discussed in past texts in some of the future conversations to keep it going without those pesky pauses.

— A new mode of conversation—think of all the places that texting can take you when you are first starting out a relationship. You can use your words, play around a bit, and even use the little emoticons to have a bit more fun. All of this will come together to help you have a lot of fun when you are meeting someone new.

Texting is a great way to get started on a new relationship, as long as you do it in the proper way. Make sure that you go through this guidebook to learn the exact steps that you should take in order to learn how to text properly and keep everything running smoothly while you are using texting.

TABLE OF CONTENTS

Introduction i

Chapter 1: Getting her number 1

Chapter 2: Getting On Her Radar 4

Chapter 3: Turning the tables 8

Chapter 4: Moving to the next level 12

Chapter 5: Call Her 15

Chapter 6: How to Handle That First Phone Call 17

Chapter 7: Post Date Texting 23

Chapter 8: 5 Things You Should Never Do While Texting 28

About the Author 33

Chapter 1

Getting her number

First things first, before you can text her you must first obtain her phone number. This can be the most challenging part for you. It is all about positioning and type of contact that you have with her. There are several ways to obtain a phone number, but all don't work.

Finding That Right approach. You must first consider where you see her and the environment that you are in. If you are in a grocery store you will definitely approach her differently than if you see her in a bar. Remember that women like men that are confident and don't appear to be playing games with her.

Approach her naturally and confidently. No matter what surroundings you are in it is important to be natural and exude confidence. Relax your mind and start a natural conversation with her. If in the grocery store you might comment about the prices of the food, or make a witty statement about not wise to shop while hungry.

These are conversation starters that match the environment that you are in. Don't strike a conversation about weather while shopping in doors. She will likely be a little put off and know it's about you wanting her number. You won't get the number or she won't answer when you text or call.

Engage her. Pay attention to her body language as you approach her and when she responds to your conversation starter. This will immediately give you clues as to whether she is interested or even wants to be bothered. Don't ignore these indicators that she gives because if you by chance see her again she will remember how annoying you were.

Once you know she is interested or responds warmly to you, take the conversation up a notch to get her to be more involved in the conversation. This may be where she asks you something or identifies with your statement and now there is commonality between the two of you.

Be direct. Women are looking for men that can be straightforward and honest about their intentions in getting to know her. In a natural way excuse yourself from the conversation and say something simple like,

"This is getting good, shall we continue this over dinner?" or "I have really enjoyed speaking with you, I would love to laugh some more over drinks." Both of these lead to exchanging of phone numbers. It also compliments her on the time and intellectual side of the interaction and not just her looks.

There are many other ways to approach a woman and get her phone number that can be fun and jovial as well. Depending on your level of assertiveness, strike up conversations that are funny and joke about obtaining her number.

Here are some things to remember to not do:

Don't ask her for phone number if your conversation lags or she seems uninterested in the conversation and you. The likelihood of you getting her number is very low.

Don't ask her for her phone number before introductions. You will probably get a very negative response from her, if she acknowledges you at all.

Don't have your friends ask for her number for you. This is extremely unattractive and will not get you the number. I know we have all seen this in movies and it seems to work, but it doesn't. A woman wants a confident man.

Chapter 2

Getting On Her Radar

Now that you have successfully gained her phone number you will need to get her "eyebrows to raise". You want her to be interested in getting to know you. Apart of sparking her interest will be staying on her radar and that will be key to your success.

Many men tend to engage in conversations where they will be agreeable with a woman. This is not necessarily the best way to spark her interest. This is definitely a way to bore her. Women are not looking for someone who will always agree with them on everything. Try having some opposite viewpoints to hers; this will be somewhat exciting for her. Women want a man that has the courage to be a little different and not like every other man.

For example; having a conversation about favorite movies and she says she loves XMEN and thinks the first one is the best one out of the series. A natural tendency may be to agree with her, but do something different and oppose that and state that XMEN first class was the best and back the opinion up. This engages her in a lighthearted debate that can become flirtatious, as you have now sparked her intellectually.

Looking at your texting game

There are several ways to create interesting text conversations with her, which will take your texting game to another level.

Match her texting style. This simply means that you will pay close attention to how she responds to you. Does she take 1 minute or 5 minutes to respond? The amount of time it takes her, you respond in a closely matched time span. This seems silly, however, when you respond too quickly this subliminally communicates that you are needy.

This neediness states that you are waiting for her to respond and this is very unattractive to a woman. Try and keep the timing and length of the texts to be closely matched without being too perfect where she thinks that you are intentionally attempting to match her.

Stay flirty. Don't engage in boring conversations such as the weather or how her day is going. Send her flirty and fun texts that catch her off guard and make her smile. This will make you stand out from others that may be pursuing her. Asking her lots of questions makes getting to know you feel like a chore or homework.

You want her to open up and the best way to do that is to catch her undivided attention. Talk about things that are random and not ordinary. For example: tell her something funny that happened to you. (Stumbling on the curb and realizing lots of people noticed) It can be something that is a little embarrassing but to her it will be interesting. You shared a moment with her as she giggles while reading your text.

Keep it casual and interesting. Make statements in the texts to her and not status quo questions. Tell her "I bet my day is topping your day right now." This may seem aloof but it grabs your attention right? It will grab hers too. This will definitely put a smile on her face even if her day is not going so well. You want to be surprising and not predictable. This mystery keeps her interested in you.

These simple ways will help you in your texting game and assist you in getting closer to the woman you want to seduce. Let's look at some examples of funny, witty and interesting texts you can send to her.

Texting Examples

"Do you know what people are saying behind your back? Nice Butt!" – This is fun and very flirty. It tells her you have a sense of humor as well as complimenting her.

"I know you are having an amazing day" – This is just a statement giving confidence that she is a terrific person and amazing is what kind of day she is having.

"I can feel you thinking about me" – Flirty and cute is what will keep you on her radar. She will smile when reading this.

"(Send her a blank text)" - This seems silly and it is but different and she will probably respond to it. It lets her know you are thinking about her.

"I bet your up to no good right now" – Bold and daring, just the shock value you want to keep her interested.

I am sure you get the idea now of what to do. Find original funny, interesting, witty, and flirty things to text that will make her smile and want to talk to you more. Don't get too sappy early on in getting to know her, but definitely poke at some things that compliment and make her laugh. Engaging her in text that still spark her intellectually and make her feel beautiful is the way to go!

Staying on her radar

Standing out and being different will get you the woman. Men that are not like every other cookie cutter man, chasing after them, intrigue women the most. Your random statements, witty comments, flirtatious verbal sparring, and fun texts will make her smile and keep her thinking about you.

What will win you the ultimate prize is all the things you haven't been doing with other women. Take a risk and be vulnerable with her and you will gain the woman that you are chasing.

Chapter 3
Turning the tables

Understanding women and the things they enjoy doing and talking about will assist you in getting her to chase you. Women are beings of emotion, and love to have fun, and talk descriptively like a good book.

Here are a few tips in how to turn the tables and get her to chase you.

Show confidence. Statements that you make in text format should exude confidence. Men that appear to be needy immediately turn off women. Example: "I know you can't stop thinking about me, I can feel your thoughts." This may seem very forward, however, it is actually a statement that puts your confidence out there. Remember balance those types of statements with other things less forward to reel her in.

Make her laugh. This is extremely important. Women prefer a man that can make her smile. If there are two men presented to her, the man that can make her laugh no matter his looks will get her attention the most.

Stay magnetic. This may be easier for some and harder for others. Remember stay engaging, enthusiastic, humorous, considerate, and intensely mysterious. This draws in the women and gets her to pay more attention to you.

Be a challenge. When she asks questions leave some mystery as to exactly what you mean. Example: "What are some things you like to do?" "I enjoy activities that keep me connected to whoever I am spending time with, how about you?" This has already raised her eyebrows as to what you really mean and appeases her more naturally sensitive side.

Don't linger. The phrase "Absence makes the heart grow fonder" is very true. Remember to respond to her texts but appear to be slightly busy even if you aren't. Keep it balanced, however, this will get her to chase you more.

Pay attention. Women respect and desire a man that pays attention to her. Acknowledge physical beauty but concentrate at first on things she says. Save a comment she said a few days prior and then briefly reference it later. Example: "I was out today and remembered you saying how great that café was so stopped and had brunch. You were right delicious!"

Master cocky and funny. Most effective way to grab a woman's attention is to make her feel good through your great sense of humor and funny antics and stories. Laughter opens her up and assists with her dropping the defense walls and letting you in.

TEXTING WOMEN

Stop doing the chasing. This is going to take some strong determination. It is in a man's nature to chase, but if you want her to chase you then you will have to be chased and not chase. Staying mysterious and funny will get her to chase you faster. The mystery and defense walls will drop with the humor. Don't let her catch right away either. Keep drawing her in.

The more you take the time to understand her, the easier it will become to get her to chase you. Remember that you are inadvertently chasing her, but she won't realize it. As you turn the tables you will be able to start more romantic dialogues with her. Be subtle at first but not too subtle that you appear to be "wimpy".

Professions of thoughts of her

Make comments such as;

"Wish you were here to see this with me,"
"Such a beautiful day to take a walk, "
"Thought about your story the other day and it made me smile."

These simple and short phrases are not too romantic but suggest that you are deeper than you appear and yet not too pushy. These statements should get her to respond in ways that make her want to spend more time with you.

You will be able to tell as the dialogue goes back and forth how quickly you can move forward with romantic gestures. This type of texting will allow you to take motes on things that she will begin to disclose to you that she likes. She might state she loves a walk on the beach at sunset, or she loves going to coffee shops and hanging out. Whatever it is take notes or save those texts so that you can use those ideas when you get to the stage of asking her out on a date.

Chapter 4

Moving to the next level

Congratulations on improving your texting game. You have successfully been communicating with her and now it's time to take it to the next level with more intentionally flirty texts.

This next step is extremely important in solidifying the mutual attraction between the two of you. She is now very intrigued by your mysterious actions and tickled by your humor. It's time to begin to prep her for you asking her out on a date.

Flirty Texts Tips

1. Women enjoy emotional and descriptive conversations. Understanding this is very essential in flirting with her. Instead of *"you're hot"*, you could say something like this, *"I love the colors you wore it really brought out your beautiful green eyes"*. Being descriptive will give her that fluttery feeling you want her to experience.

2. Women like a man that can be both a great conversation leader and can let her lead. This is a balancing act.

Allow her to ask you questions and answer in a way that leaves her in control still. Listen intently so that you can playback what she says creatively later.

3. Make fun statements, not always silly over the top funny. Many times it's the witty statements that really will catch her attention. The gut wrenching funny comes later. Just keep her smiling and giggling.

4. Non-verbal communication still happens, even in texts. Many times her non-verbal communication gives you clues as to how interested she is or how much she thinks about you. So pay attention to what you are reading.

5. Try some friendly and flirtatious teasing. This would be softly teasing while complimenting at the same time. Be careful not to tease too heavily as that could turn her off and chase her away.

6. Tell her your observations of her. Don't be afraid. She enjoys hearing your thoughts. So go for it. Tell her how intelligent and creative you think she is. And back your statement up with an example from conversation.

7. Remember to not over compliment, this will make you sound fake and not sincere in your interest in her as a person. Make compliments naturally as you are in conversation with her.

Examples of Flirty Texts

"Good Morning Beautiful", this tells her you are thinking of her even at the start of the day. She probably has n't done much yet, so now you inserted yourself as a th ought.

"I feel the warmth from your smile." This is telling her you remember her smile.

"You're making it hard for me to sleep?" This will engage her and intrigue her because she will want to know why. She will also think this corny and cute.

Using Emoticons to Flirt

It's not always what you say but the timing and the small cute indicators that show your interest in her. With texting you should utilize the emoticons that are available to you.

A wink, a rose, smile, heart, or even gestures can get your point across very well. She will appreciate the small indicators as well. Harder to say the wrong thing when you are just sending a wink.

Don't overdo it, however, sending a wink will let her know you're thinking about her. She will appreciate the non-verbal communication via text as well.

Chapter 5
Call Her

While texting can be a great way to get in contact with a woman without bothering her and without the stress of talking to her, this should not be the only way to communicate in order to get your point across.

The texting can be saved for getting to know each other and sharing each other interests on your own time, but there will be times when you will need to actually put away the texting and call up the girl you are interested in.

This is going to be a daunting task for some. They might like the security that is behind the texting since they do not have to feel awkward about it all and they will be able to think about their responses before sending them off.

Yes, texting is a very secure form of communication, but it is not the only one. Just think of it this way, how awkward is it going to be if you have not talked to a girl since you got her number when you show up for the first date? It is going to be much worse than trying to hold out.

If you would like to be a gentleman, take the time to call her up. She is going to appreciate the effort, don't think that she is not going to notice that you put in this effort, and she is going to feel much more at ease when it is time to go to the date. Do not just do it all through text. While it is fine to send over a little bit of a text as a confirmation, this should not occur until after you have had an actual conversation about the time and location of your first date.

While you might prefer the chance of just texting all of this information to the woman, it is going to work against. You. She will see you as a person who is unconfident and will go into the first date with this.

She will then hold a lot of this against you, even if she is not meaning to, so that you are going to have to work extra hard in order to convince her of something else. Of course, if you try too hard at that, you will come off looking like a jerk and this is not going to work very well for you either.

Just by making a good call to her in order to say hello, see how their day was, and then making some plans for the first date you will be able to show that you are actually interested in the girl. Do not worry about not sounding confident and strong. Instead just try to take it easy and show some interest in the woman. With the right attitude and just doing your best, you are already setting yourself up for a great date with this girl.

Chapter 6
How to Handle That First Phone Call

Many guys who get a number from a girl are only going to spend their time talking with the girl using text. While this is a way to go, if you really want to stand out, you need to make a call to the girl as well. It is going to take some confidence in order to make this call rather than hiding behind some texts.

It is also a big risk to try and think of things on your toes rather than getting some time to think about what you would like to say. Most men are going to be worried about what they should say and how do they make the conversation last rather than let it going flat. Follow some of these tips for that first phone call so it can go off without a hitch and you can get that date.

The Pre-Call:

Before you start calling the girl, you should make sure that your game is on. Sometimes practicing out the things that you want to say before you call the girl, or at least having some sort of list present can help you to get this done easier without as many worries. Write some of these things down and then have a practice conversation a few times before you call.

This can really help if you have the jitters about talking to her and can keep you from slipping up as much during the conversation. Of course the conversation is not going to go exactly the way that you practiced it, but at least you have a little practice and are able to feel a bit more confident before starting.

Work on your voicemail

In some cases, the girl may give you a call first. If this does happen, you want to make sure that she is going to be interested in leaving you a voicemail. Have the message on your voicemail be funny or cute or even leave a little brain teaser. This allows you to have something to talk about when you give her a call back, which will avoid some of the awkward pauses that often come with the phone conversation.

When you should call

It is a good idea to call her at some point, but you will also want to make sure that she is available and that you will not be bugging her and you want to be able to ask her out on a date with plenty of time for preparations so it does not sound like it was planned last minute. Some of the things that you can keep in mind when you are looking to call a girl include:

Right after getting the phone number—it is sometimes a good idea to call a girl right after you have gotten her number. This helps you to stay in her mind a bit longer and you can just start it out with making sure that you got the right number. If possible, start the conversation where you left off when you last met to keep things interesting.

Sunday to Wednesday—the best time to call is in between these days. The rest of the days are the ones when people are the busiest and she will probably be out doing something else.

You are going to seem a little pathetic if you are calling and wanting to talk for a long time on a Saturday night. You should also call earlier in the week if you are planning on asking her out so that she has plenty of time to have a clear schedule and can come out with you.

Send a text ahead of time—text the girl before you decide to call her to see if she is busy or available to talk for a while. This allows you to know that she is free and that you will not be bothering her as much as you would just calling on the fly.

Of course, another fun thing to do is wait for her to text you because you will then automatically know that she is free and you will not be bothering her. When you receive that text, reply back that you are going to call her in a few seconds. Wait a minute or two and then call. Then she is expecting you to call and you can get right in the conversation.

Set up your time early—you can even set up the time that you would like to call her as you are getting her number. You can tell her that you would be free on Monday night at 7 pm and see if that time will work for her. This allows you to have a free time to call and can get rid of the anxiousness you might be feeling about her not answering the phone at all.

Ready for the call

It is fine to be a bit nervous during this part of the process, but do not let the ring's on the other end scare you. Some men might pick up the phone, but they are so nervous that they hope it is going to go straight to voicemail so that they do not have to talk to the woman. Take a big breath while you are calling and then start to think in a more positive manner.

When it is the first time that you are calling, it is not a good idea to hang up the phone until it is done. This means that you either need to have a conversation with the girl or you need to leave a voicemail.

Hopefully you are able to get in touch with the girl so that you can have a conversation and get to know each other, but at least with a voicemail you are providing incentive for her to get back in contact with you.

If you do end up leaving a voicemail, make sure that you are doing it in the right way in order to entice her to give you a call back. You can leave almost anything that you would like ranging from a question you would like her to answer, saying something that is kind of crazy, or just mention your last conversation to pique her interest.

You can also make the conversation sweet and to the point. Just make sure that you are not just asking her to call you back when she has the time. This does not put a limit on when she can call you and it could take a week or could be when you are at work and the phone tag will begin. If you have a certain time that would work best for you, tell her that to make things easier.

In some cases, the woman might not be able to call you back for a few days. She might have something going on or might not have realized that there was a message for her. If you do not get a call back, you should wait a few days before trying to call her again.

She picks it up

In some cases, the woman is going to actually pick up the phone when you call her. Do not take this as a bad sign. It was exactly what you wanted. But if she does pick up, make sure that you have something to say. You do not want to make the conversation awkward or end up hanging up the phone on her. This goes back to having a few ideas ready and written down so if you get stuck, then you are able to help yourself out.

You also need to make sure that you are able to keep the conversation going for a period of time; no one wants to just have a conversation that is a question and then a few word answer. Try to talk about something that interests you as well as her or imagine that you are talking to one of your good friends.

TEXTING WOMEN

The woman is going to respond in kind and then the conversation will keep on going for a long period of time. Of course, you also need to make a good way to end the conversation since it is not going to go on forever. You could say that you have something going on that you need to go do or even set up the date to end out the call.

As you can see, the phone call with the girl does not have to be as scary as you think. She is as worried about how this is all going to go as you are so just take a deep breath and have some fun. It does not have to be tedious and can even be an extension off the foundation you have worked on with the texting. Plus it is going to put you in a much better light with this woman which can make the whole date go so much better.

Chapter 7
Post Date Texting

First date should have given you a pretty good look at whether you would like to spend more time with this girl and get to know her or if you are ready to look somewhere else for some help. This chapter is going to spend some time on what you should do when you are done with your date.

You want to meet again

In some cases, you might find that the date went as well as you could have hoped. You both had a lot of fun, the girl was even better than you thought she might be to begin with, and you want to go out with her again.

This is great news because it means that all of your hard work is paying off and you did not waste all of that time texting or trying to call the girl in vain. You hope that all of your dates are going to turn out this way, and even if it does not turn out to be something that is for the long term, you at least want to see this girl for a few more dates.

When you want to go out on another date with this girl, you have to keep up with the texting and talking to her. Make sure that you are not being creepy with too much contact, but you can do a little bit more now to find out if she is interested in you still and wants to continue on with dating some more. Hopefully the two of you like each other the same so that this process is a bit easier to do.

Make sure to ask to see if she made it home safely and to tell her goodnight. You can send her a text once you get home to check in or you can just let her know to text you when she gets home. This shows that you really care about her and want to be there for her. It's a nice little touch that is going to keep her interested and may open the door to more later on if you wish.

Finally, make sure that you let her know that you would like to get together again. Sometimes a girl may be worried about if you had fun or not and may be a bit nervous about making the next move. If you let them know right away that you are interested, you can keep things going much easier.

Date was OK, but you'll give it a shot.

The girl is fun, you have had a great time getting to know her through text, but the date was really bad and you are not sure whether you should do it all again. But you decide that the issue might be your nerves or hers or maybe even the location where you picked out for dinner and so you would like to give it a bit more of a chance.

This is a great idea because it allows you to still get in another date and perhaps it will be a bit more fun and relaxed.

When this happens to you, you can still carry on through the texting like you would above. You might want to think of a better place to go for a date, or if you were the one to choose, see where she would like to go.

Chances are she will pick somewhere she is the most comfortable at and the date might go so much better. You can even use the texting to joke a bit about the last date, saying something that will get you both to look back fondly on the date with some laughter rather than wincing because it was so terrible.

Whether or not the date went fine, you should make sure that she feels special and keep on with some of the steps that were listed above in terms of still texting her and getting to know her. It is still important that you carry on a conversation and get to know each other, even if it might turn into just another date or two.

You are not interested

There are going to be times when you meet what you think is an amazing girl and then you go on a date and find that it was horrible, she spent all of that time not making eye contact or talking about herself, and you just do not want to put yourself through all of that again. It is important to take some defensive actions right away to stop with the dating and so you can move on to someone else.

Of course, this becomes more complicated when you find out the girl is still interested in you.

First off, do not lead the girl on. If you do not like her, do not spend that time still talking with her, promising dates that will never happen, and still acting like you really care about her. You might think that you are being nice, but in reality, you are hurting her feelings more than ever.

Find a way to let her know gently that you are not interested in continuing the relationship and that you do not want to see her again. It might seem harsh, but it is much better to do this early on rather than letting her think there is still something available.

Some of the things that you should do in order to make sure that this goes on the right level to avoid hard feelings and to end it right away include:

Be direct—do not go around the bush. Get right to your point instead of trying to flower it all up. The extra words and being nice will make it worse.

Be truthful—making up reasons that the date did not go well is not a good idea. Just let them know that you are not really interested into the date and you can add a reason, but keep it truthful.

Be general—you need be truthful, but you do not need to go into details about what happened. If you list all of the things that went wrong in the date, you are just going to seem mean. Be general in your discussion.

Be firm—you are probably going to feel a bit guilty about breaking up with this girl, but don't let that pressure you. It is just going to be harder if you hold on and let it continue in this direction. Show some respect—thank the girl for her time and that you appreciate the time she spent with you.

Always be polite even if the girl is not as nice. It is hard to be rejected and she might not feel the best when you break up, especially if she had a great time. Remember this and be polite.

Keep this short—you do not have to go on for a long time with this. You just had one date so keep it short and sweet.

Chapter 8

5 Things You Should Never Do While Texting

It is sometimes difficult to know what you should and should not do when you are texting a woman. It is confusing to know what steps you are supposed to take in order to get the next date. Here are some of the top things that you should avoid if you want to make sure that you are getting the most out of your texting time with this new girl.

1. Do not give up too quickly

Texting is sometimes difficult to do with a new girl and many guys are going to give up too quickly. They might find that if they do not get a text back for a bit or the reply is brief, that the girl is just not interested. There are many reasons why a girl is going to not reply right away.

You must remember that she has a job and responsibilities too and cannot sit by the phone all day long. A girl will tell you if she is not interested so give her a bit of time and do not come off as too needy in the process.

Give the girl a bit of time to get back to you. She is going to let you know what works the best for her needs and she is going to get back to you soon. Just because you work the night shift and are more available during the day does not mean that she is ignoring you. Most likely, she is at work and will text you later on. The trick is that you both need to find a time that you are both free with your schedules, which might take some time in the beginning, and then it will be easier. But if you give up too quickly, you will find that you will never get to know how well things could go.

2. Texting too much

Yes, you are not supposed to give up on this girl too quickly, but things can also go the other way and you can become too needy. Writing out one simple text during the day and then leaving it there until that night when she may have more time is fine, but sending 20 desperate texts and driving her nuts is not a good thing either.

You should try to keep the texting ration 1 to 1. Of course, you do not need to count your texts and make sure it is at this amount, but you should be able to tell it is pretty close to this and going to be like a conversation. Getting too far from this ratio is going to make you sound desperate and needy and that is not a good start to the conversation.

TEXTING WOMEN

Never look like you are going to be too needy to a girl. She wants to feel like she is important in your life, but she does not want to feel like you are going to be bugging her all of the time. She does have her own life and at this point of the game, she does not want to feel like she has to give it all up for a guy she just met.

You would not want a girl who is really clingy to you before the first date because you know that things will just get worse the longer you two are together. The girl is going to feel the same way and if you are texting her too much, she might decide not to take the chance on the first date with you.

3. Being serious all of the time

There is always a time and a place to have those serious conversations but usually texting is not the place to do it and especially before the first date has even occurred. Being serious over texting can be tiring and nobody wants to do it. You should keep all of the serious conversations to when you are actually together. Keep the texting to some fun and light conversations so that you can have a bit of fun.

Save the serious stuff for later on. You are in the beginning of the relationship and have no idea how far it is going to go. At this point, you are just trying to figure out how to get this girl on the first date with you. You do not need to get into the really serious things all of a sudden and scare her away.

Plus it is hard to tell what is serious and what is sillier when you are on text so it is best to leave that alone at this point. Just have some fun and save that serious stuff for when the two of you can be together.

4. Not texting women

If this is the first woman you have ever texted besides your mother, you are going to find that the issue with texting too much is going to be more common than you think. This is because you are not used to doing it and it is going to be hard to figure out what is normal or not.

Of course, this does not mean that you need to go out and get the numbers of 20 other women and try to date all of them; this is just going to cause a lot of problems down the road. Rather, maybe find a few women from work you can start a friendship with or get in touch with some other girls that you have no romantic interest in and practice.

If you have texted with other women, you will find that it is much easier to have a conversation with the woman you are trying to get a date out of at this time.

5. Missing out on the big pictures

Sometimes, you may forget the way of texting a girl. You might get wrapped in with some idle talking and then you will forget about the big picture. Of course, this big picture is going to get the girl to get together with you through the texting.

You do not need to spend the whole time texting the girl doing planning and logistics and having some fun with texting is fine. But you do not want to be six months down the road with this and still not on the first date. You want to be more direct and get the girl to be interested and ready to be on the first date with you. Keep this in mind with your texts and this can help you get on the right track to setting up that first date with this girl.

Keep with that big picture and try to show the girl how much fun you can have with her. This is a girl you want to impress so missing out on that and showing her how wonderful you can be is not a smart thing. Take the time to remember all of this and work towards getting together and making a great first impression at that first date is important.

As you can see, the advice for doing well on the first date is not that hard to do. Just make sure that you are working to really impress her but that you are not becoming too needy. She wants to know that you are going to be a lot of fun, but that you will also let her have her own life in all of this and will not become too much of a hassle, at least unitl way down the line.

But you are worried about the here and now and do not need to worry about that part for now. Just show her how amazing you are now and use these steps in order to have a great time.

About the Author

Felicia Vine is an author & relationship expert, born in Italy in a small city called Otranto. At 16 she moved to the USA with her parents, where she graduated from the University of Rochester with degree in psychology.

Now she is working as a relationship consultant and freelance writer, writing articles on relationship topics for several online resources.

In her spare time, Felicia writes books to enlighten the public on relationship and sex topics. She has also authored several romance and erotica novels.

Now she lives in New York with her boyfriend and small Yorkshire terrier, Allie.

Made in the USA
Middletown, DE
24 December 2016